WHAT RICH PEOPLE DON'T DO

"15 SECRETS OF MILLIONAIRES"

TABLE OF CONTENTS

Introduction 1

CH 1: They Don't Spend Money Anyhow Rather They Save 5

CH 2: They Don't Develop A Fear Mindset Rather A Wealth Mindset 7

CH 3: They Don't Own Much 11

CH 4: They Don't Fail To Use Leverage To Make Money Quick 14

CH 5: They Don't Waste Time On Irrelevant Things 21

CH 6: They Don't Avoid Risks 25

CH 7: They Don't Pursue A Goal Without A Driven Purpose 31

CH 8: They Do Not Blame Anyone For Loss, Mistakes, Or Weakness ... 38

CH 9: They Do Not Have A Weak Determination 46

CH 10: They Never Fail To Get Along With People 49

CH 11: They Do Not Invest Wrongly 52

CH 12: They Don't Occupy Their Mind With Misery And Depression ... 56

CH 13: They Don't Ignore The Importance Of Sowing Seeds 60

CH 14: They Don't See Failure As The End Of The Road 64

CH 15: They Do Not Hesitate To Take Needed Action To Retain
    Momentum 69

Conclusion 72

INTRODUCTION

With some intimate, tightly guarded financial principles, each millionaire might amass his wealth. Millionaires become millionaires because they know about the secrets of money-making and holding, but you seldom see a millionaire publicly revealing his/her secrets of wealth generation. They would simply not encourage you to peek into their lives to glimpse their carefully disguised secrets.

Since I was curious about the millionaire's secrets, I did a lot of research. I concluded that many people strive to become millionaires; nevertheless, the wealth formation principles of a few works.

First, a millionaire puts a lot of effort into making his/her financial aspirations become a reality. At the same time, not everybody who works hard becomes a millionaire. For example, the idea of inventing and selling useful goods is quite lucrative; however, only a few entrepreneurs can succeed.

Millionaires are also individuals whose financial secrets are closely guarded. Many people mistake that a person can become rich as long as they have a job with fat pay and requisite qualifications, but that's not exactly right.

Millionaires don't get well-paid jobs. Indeed many educated people searching for work are people who wonder whether they can make their fortunes themselves. Do you want to gain great wealth? You must then get rid of your fears, create trust, and learn to fight for your rights.

If your ambition is to win millions, start working on it right away. No one is born a millionaire. Most present millionaires were as poor as church mice when their financial journeys began. Millionaires have the potential to make a huge deal of the little they have. Therefore the first step in becoming wealthy is to reflect on the riches you already possess, not on the one-day success you dream of. Create your self-knowledge, and such awareness will still benefit you. Only if you have the appropriate skills will you perform well in a specific area. Similarly, if you want to boost your financial situation, you have to learn your thinking's essence and trends.

Would you like to tap into millionaires' secrets?

Do you want to solve the mystery of how millions of people make so much money?

Millionaires have made great efforts to make their dreams come true. A millionaire can hardly be found to relax or surf the internet forever before the TV. They work hard to safeguard their financial status.

Millionaires are common people with strange dreams. What distinguishes them from the rest of the population is that they can achieve their dreams. You must learn millionaires' great secrets to build up wealth, to find the way to your passions, and to rejoice in a fruitful and successful life.

It will take you a long time to access trustworthy and valuable knowledge. The best information sources are generally the most popular. You can read books, inspire and coach conversations, or just surround yourself with people and instruments that can provide good tactics, tips, and techniques.

The desire to be driven is also a key tactic for most millionaires and the wealthy. Their capacity to learn has enabled them to grow in wealth and emotional, social, and intellectual terms. Take the time to let your learning disappear and look at mistakes and losses. Don't let them get you down. Instead, look back and note the improvements you need to make to your plans.

It all involves taking the necessary steps to advance your plans and to achieve results. For example, you want debt-free and financial freedom. You should prepare for debt and financial stability and take steps to save money and pay your bills on time.

If you've felt a bit discouraged or recently, perhaps it's time to change your point of view. You need the secrets of millionaires to boost your confidence and inspire you to face the challenges ahead. You need to be motivated to meet your goals.

You have to start looking for any knowledge that could help you to succeed. Several resources can be consulted for details and facts. You ought to read some books or hear people inspired by their version of success formulas. You can also view videos online and download audiobooks to help you use your successful journey.

Write down your hopes, ambitions, and expectations on a sheet of paper. Write down actions to achieve one goal after another on a separate sheet. This helps you figure out what results you expect and what needs to be done to make life a success.

You must take these steps and start doing so. Take small measures every day. Create and implement an action plan. In contrast to common assumptions, fast-track systems are entirely unstable pillars of success and prosperity. Even millionaires have to sweat it at the beginning. That is why you must learn and take them every day from their experiences.

Are you tired of a failed life?

Do you want to know what it takes to make the most of your life?

Do you want the knowledge that will change your life forever?

If it's a big yes, you can get your hands on millionaires' secrets and learn what it takes in life to be successful. This GUIDE features 15 top secrets of millionaires that can help you achieve and succeed in your dreams. You should find the tools to help you do this if you feel you need these millionaires' secrets to find more ways to succeed.

Let's get started

CHAPTER 1:

They Don't Spend Money Anyhow Rather They Save

We usually think of private jets, exclusive yachts, and mansions by the ocean when we think about how rich people spend money, but the rich don't spend all their money on anything like this when you think about it. Honestly, buying this is only throwing money away, and they can also collect it all into a large pile and burn. Rich people are usually intelligent with their expenses - like Warren Buffett.

I'm sure all of you have heard of Mr. Warren Buffett - the biggest wealth accumulator in history. A great book I'm reading tells the story of his private jet journey to a meeting. I didn't think that impressive.

Until I read and learned how Berkshire Hathaway owned a company that rented private jets for such opportunities, now that's clever. He has no jet collecting dust when he doesn't use it, and the crew works and earns him money until he has to fly anywhere and makes a phone call. Very nice.

Now that's what I mean by rich people who wisely spend their money. If such a purchase happens, money is not thrown away, and it has been invested, which in turn generates even more money.

Now the rest of us should learn something - and I'm not just gathering money in some businesses - that's not my thing. I mean to be clever with expenses. It's nice to buy yourself something extravagant - a big chocolate block for some of us, a private jet for others. However, what you need to remember is to plan the expenses.

The rich set t goals and objectives for themselves. Most rich people achieve exceptionally efficiently, not by chance, but by sheer determination and careful planning.

The rich don't spend money to waste, and they plan every expense carefully – just as they count the dollars that come in, the intelligent will also count the dollars going out. This is what we, aspiring wealthy, should do; we should emulate the rich's efforts and actions, provided that, of course, they work.

Strategies to save money invented by rich people

Rich people are using special strategies to save and invest money. You, too, can be on a path to wealth development by learning what they do and copying them.

1. First, pay yourself. This is THE money-making strategy. Since the beginning of time, rich people have done this. It makes perfect sense, and if you establish this habit, the results will surprise you.

What most people do to save – which is completely backward – usually works like that.

- They are paid for their job or business
- They save anything left over
- They take a certain, predetermined amount into their savings (usually about 10 percent)
- They pay and live their bills (i.e., spend money)

Do you see the difference in money-saving strategies? First, wealthy people pay themselves. No matter what, they're depositing into their account every month.

CHAPTER 2:

They Don't Develop A Fear Mindset Rather A Wealth Mindset

A millionaire way of thinking means focusing. Millionaires focus very well on what they plan and what they want to achieve. For them, it's not how well you plan but how successful you are in the performance of tasks.

The next big thing a focused person has is the direction. When you have defined your life goal and know your passions, this is the key to your success. Knowing all of your plans gives you guidance and meaning to your life.

This is what drives you to do great things in life and gives you passion. It takes more than a dream to get what you want. You have to take action and practice yourself. Make and follow your mission statement and the purpose and direction of your actions.

Continue to visualize what you want to do. Motivate yourself and mobilize to move and get there. If it means you must fully engage your heart and yourself to realize and achieve more, do it. Concrete actions help to keep your direction and achieve the best for you and your family.

The way we are motivated, inspired, and passionate about successful people. These are people who are flexible and open to new opportunities and better guidance. Choose a route where you can unlock your hidden abilities and use all your ability to achieve more and to achieve higher than anticipated goals. You must also stimulate your current actions to think out of the box and leave your comfort zone.

Many people don't plan to move and just don't know what or where they are going. One important feature of a millionaire's thinking is well defined and set goals and priorities, even if it only means sacrificing and negotiating to achieve his objectives. Millionaires don't wait for opportunities to knock at their doors. Instead, these opportunities are created, and chances are taken to earn money.

The millionaire mindset is convinced;

- If they do not, they can try again and again
- Losing their stance repels the wealth
- Understands that at all times, anybody can succeed
- Thinking and planning is key to success in the future
- Faith in their abilities is the driving force to achieve higher objectives.

You don't have to be a millionaire to think like this, but you can better start changing this life now if you want to become one.

Poverty starts with the mind, they say. You can't get a poor mind anywhere. That is why you must begin to ease your thinking by incorporating some of the millionaires' success secrets in your life. You will see how these secrets differ, especially in how you think, react, and feel about your present and future situations.

The important thing to focus on at the beginning of your successful journey is your thinking. You have to change your paradigm. This shift in thinking can include a new focus on your motivation, efforts, time, and other resources to achieve your goals. So you ought to do it:

Write your goals on a piece of paper first. Contemplate these objectives and see whether they are specific, manageable, effective, rational, and time-bound. If you don't follow these skills, you must begin to tweak your objectives.

The next thing you have to do is obtain useful and credible information that reveals millionaires' secrets. These can be found from self-help books like this one you read, listen to a motivational speaker, and encircle yourself with successful people.

Always take notes and remember the main facts and information you have obtained from them to return it if you have forgotten something. Create a vision board that will make you see what is in front of you. This is a great motivating tool that will further improve your drive and change your thinking course.

Let yourself be inspired by others. Search for inspiring resources, guides, and people. Seek people who can be your role models and who can provide a great deal of wisdom on your journey to success. It's not easy to develop a "rich" mindset. Sometimes you may even need some assistance. The above tips are just some ways of helping you think for the greater good rather than focusing on your current and past situations.

Millionaires think big—big millions. Ordinary people don't think big. To find out how to do something, it is best to start small but don't get caught up in challenges. If you had a million dollars, identify your ideal situation. What would you and your associates invest in if you had 10 million? Work to that end!

A millionaire is mostly a matter of mental behavior. If you want to become one, you will. I prepare you for this shift in this chapter to compare the attitudes of "millionaires" and "normal individuals." I'm just using millions and ordinary people as symbols of how active and prosperous people think.

Their differences in mental behavior do not make cars or shoe brands. There's no social snobbishness here. Think like one if you want to be a millionaire. You don't need the car or the shoes, but you do need the mind.

Today's economic system presents our financial stability with many challenges, but there are many ways to make a buck nowadays, even a fortune. Most of us are our own worst hindrance. It's time for us to start thinking big to meet our potential.

Put yourself in an environment that is favorable. Discover a cheerful place that gives you a good feeling. This allows you to do some productive brainstorming. Brainstorming is simple, but brainstorming that leads to results is the key.

Keep down all negativism. They're against you if they're not for you. Stay out of the pessimists. Other negativism could and will cause you to fall. Misery is a company, and distressed persons tend to push other people or reflect their sadness.

Surround yourself with favorable people, preferably people with the same objectives and concerns. The comfort and favorable strengthening of others can be an important asset for your success.

Your plan is your key component. Pattern a plan up. This is the first step towards genuine action. It doesn't look like your trouble, or anyone else's just talking about an idea. Once you draw up a plan, you will have opened the first door to start your new work.

Don't be afraid of having big hopes. Neither will anyone else believe in you if you don't believe in yourself. It's important to understand that you can simply do anything you think about. Draw a bead on it if you have a passion for something. It could only be your key to a successful future. There is absolutely no time to be scared or tired of trying new and potentially fruitful things.

CHAPTER 3:

They Don't Own Much

Do rich people own a lot? I first heard the idea of my mentor summed up my confusion. Hey, come back. At the moment, the notion that the rich are without owners made no sense to me, but I soon realized that this is one of the most important principles, as important as the 'Second Money Rule,' in creating wealth.

Instead of owning income-generating properties, cars, bank accounts, purchasing food, or paying school fees on your behalf, you have the option of buying property and doing business regularly on behalf of a corporation.

By forming one, you effectively become an employee or representative of the organization—everything you do in your name as an individual. For example, your credit card would not have your name imprinted on it but your company's name. For real estate, the same occurs. Purchasing or selling property happens in the name of your cooperation, not your name. You are simply acting as the facilitator of each contract.

As a result, wealth creators typically have very few personal names. They are the true owners of their assets that generate income and, thus, wealth. So what exactly is a partnership or a business?

This is something that, when I started, puzzled me. It's not a factory or a retail company. It's not a big building or a brand name, nor is it a community of professionals with a specialty service. It's just a legally registered government paper. Anyone can set up a business. That is the beauty of the method. No physical thing needs to be produced to begin a company. The paperwork is what you're expected to do.

A business makes playing the game of wealth formation much simpler. A person can get into a corporate atmosphere so much better than an individual can. This is how wealthy people have done it for hundreds of years.

A business or corporation is based on two main reasons:

1. Benefits from tax:

As an employee, you pay government taxes first, and then you survive on what is left (post-tax dollars), and the more you get discounts or hard stuff, the more the government gets. Tax is a big expense that should be reduced as much as possible legally.

This is where the firm comes in.

First of all, the last income is taxed, which means that the government just shares the last income. By living on dollars before taxes, you benefit. For instance, mortgage costs, vacations, car payments, and food are called company expenditures. Only after eliminating these charges will revenue be paid.

Individuals: earn, pay tax, live

Live taxes:

Secondly, South Africa taxes corporations at 28%. If your tax rate reaches 28 percent, you will gain as a person. Business in a company at lower tax rates minimizes the tax expenses, meaning you have more income-generating asset resources.

2. Protective security

Partnership's second big advantage is investor and litigation immunity. Let's face it. You own and handle everything under your name. Your name is a direct path to your money and properties. If a court has proved their claims, every one can simply sue you.

You don't have much in a business, but you do—the ultimate defensive form. Deleting your assets will take a hard time if someone wants to sue you for any alleged indiscretion. Furthermore, depending on how you organize your company, corporations will add different security types to your assets.

In short, collaboration exists not only for the wealthy but for everyone who wants to own and retain their income-generating properties.

CHAPTER 4:

They Don't Fail To Use Leverage To Make Money Quick

Does it seem unworkable to use somebody else's money to buy something for yourself? It should not; it always happens. Have you borrowed your car anyway? You taped into the money of others in the bank) to purchase a car. How much better if somebody else paid for you already?

You do that by investing in real estate. Instead of using money from others to collect extra costs, you're using money from other people (banks) to buy the house, and you're using money from others (your tenants) to pay by renting the property more than you own. After all, expenses are paid, the revenue generated by the property is the cash flow of the property. Simply put, this is the strength of the leverage.

Too many people believe they need to save a large down payment before the bank leases money to purchase the property. This is not true. There are some ways to obtain funding without making a down payment. The best way to start is to buy your first property and then use your equity to buy more.

Equity is the difference between the value and the owing. If you own a $100,000 property and have an $80,000 mortgage on the property, your shareholding is $20,000. The use of the equity in one property to buy another exerts the power of leverage. Leverage helps to improve the wealth process. The use of leverage maximizes your purchasing capacity. It's the perfect way to buy land, build healthy cash flows, and gain value.

Assessment is an asset's value over some time. If you take your $20,000 equity and use it as a down payment to buy one more house, then you would benefit from the cash flow of the two properties, rather than one.

You would also appreciate two properties instead of one. Real estate properties increased on average between 3 and 8 percent per year. You use leverage, but not entirely, to buy one property. How much quicker will your wealth grow if you are using it to buy only $5,000 each to buy four properties rather than using your $20,000 to buy another property?

The appreciation and cash flow of four more properties would boost your wealth rather than one. Believe it or not, you too can take control of your financial life by acquiring real estate.

Besides being one of the only investments globally, you can buy property revenue and earnings from the strength of leverage and receive some of the highest available tax breaks. Compared to stocks and other assets, gains can be tax-delayed or even tax-free!

The government can use every windfall through a 1031 exchange process in your next real estate investment. It feels good to make money and not to pay the lion's tax.

Real estate can also create wealth in any economic climate. When the real estate market is up, rapid turnover (flips) of investment can generate significant immediate gains. If the price falls, there are more opportunities for buying assets at a lower cost due to advance, motivated sellers, and sales financing.

If interest rates are very low, you can purchase more assets for your buck. More guests are encouraged to rent apartments at higher rates, which means higher rental prices. The increasing demand makes your property a cash flow cow. The power of leverage is remarkable, and you can start to use it today. Whether you own a home with equity, or are willing to buy your first deal, allow leverage power to save you from successful real estate investment.

The Greek Archimedes once said, "Give me a lever and a place to stand, and I could move the world." He understood that a lever is a means of increasing your strength over natural boundaries. He also knew that the higher the lever, the stronger the force. The lever may, unfortunately, be a second cliché, a two-edged sword for the uninformed. Unwise used the incorrect leverage can't only increase your upside; it works efficiently on the downside and can raise your risk.

Most believe they understand leverage believe that only borrowed money is used to purchase (dye) stocks or use a mortgage to buy a house or an investment property (safe). My father is the first display of your leverage, but his sad account does not invalidate my premise that your rich program is critical to leverage if you want to be truly rich.

Knowing fully well that a lever is just one way to increase your power, and you should use it all wisely, and there are three different leverage modes. There is the leverage of money and time, and I ask you to show me a rich man who didn't use at least one. (I don't know movie stars getting a photo of $20 million and athletes making millions of dollars a year over a few years.

It's a difference between a McDonald's counter-employer, 6 USD an hour, and an advocate, 300 USD an hour? Not as much as you think. When you both don't, they're not paid. Their income is limited to how many hours they are working.

Even worse than it seems, personal income is paid at the highest tax rates for every form of personal income. If you rely on your income alone, you are like an upstream salmon swam, holding a barber. One aspect of the rich strategy is to be personally poor or modest, enabling a minimum of highly taxable personal income.

You will make money even if your money doesn't work for you, your staff will work for you, your partners work for you, and your money will work for you to duplicate, triple and long tasks.

Let us look at the various types of leverage:

1: Money Leverage: The old cliché says money is needed to make money, but that's not your money.

All wealthy people use leverage to purchase a mortgage for a much better house than their savings. Efficient real estate investors will not become wealthy unless they borrow money to purchase properties. Banks are not only on the monetary market but also produce leverage, and in this situation, the government is your friend.

Unlike purchasing margin stocks, no government body enforces margin-call laws against you in real estate. When the real estate hits a soft spot (as in recent times), and your home's valued value falls below your mortgage balance, you don't need to borrow money to cover the lender. Do your shopping, and it will remain yours. This is because the real estate sector has successfully lobbied.

2: How about rich businessmen such as Bill Gates? He used a lot of leverage, increased his earnings and his company's safety, and assessed his properties. By selling some of his stock, he raised many investors' money and used it to grow his business.

The overwhelming majority of his $60 billion property is his remaining corporate stock. This is leverage. When asked how wealthy he was, Ted Turner said, "I must be really rich, I owe a lot of money."

There is good debt and poor debt. The debt of the customer is always poor. Debt is always bad. Corporate debt, if you use it right, is healthy debt. It's okay to buy assets that produce enough cash to fulfill the debt and then some. Therefore, I would like to clarify whether a debt is a good debt or a poor debt.

Bad Debt

- Money to buy something which melts when used, leaving debt alone — just like a holiday.
- Money borrowed to buy the money-eating alligator. It could be a vacation or a motor home or the bigger home you live in (which is the best argument for buying a smaller home than your credit score would qualify you for). If you redefine "asset," it's not an asset since it's a negative cash flow alligator.
- Cash lent to buy a generally depreciating commodity, such as a car or ship. I am speaking of real depreciation, which means a genuine loss in the market, not phantom depreciation, such as tax deductions on the property if it is good.

Healthy Debt

I will not list because there is just a good kind of debt - money you lend to work to create income-producing assets and generate enough cash flows to systematically minimize the principal.

More money is invested

The money lent is not the only kind of leverage. In situations where a contractor sells some of its equities to fund the business by selling private or public securities to his company, it uses the cash leverage.

If he could sell 10 percent of his business and generate cash that doubles his company's revenue and profit, it would be nice, and he would be a fool not to do so. He is richer because his remaining stock value grows when he owns 100% of the stock and has worked cash for his company's investment. Such cash is a reinforcing lever.

I have known business people who work 12 to 15 hours a day because they don't trust other people to do their job properly. This reflects more on the contractor than on his staff. If she is professional, let her do her work, and if she is not, get rid of her and hire her.

These contractors do not grasp the concept of People Leverage. If they hadn't had time to do so, a clever business would recruit people to do what they can or wouldn't do, to do everything they can and provide leadership and strategic guidance for their business.

Personal leverage is not only beneficial, but its absence will sign the death warrant for a business. Nobody can do anything. When he tries, he burns down and doesn't have time to secure or lose anything that cracks and destroys the business or gets so lost in the details that he can't keep abreast of his industry progress and misses possibilities.

CEO's mentality

Business people who use people can quickly become very wealthy by establishing an additional team of real managers who know their skills and are allowed to use them. A real CEO (Chief Executive Officer) will clarify what the business goals are to his staff, identify a strategy and battle plan, endorse the plan and encourage it to function according to its guidelines and budget, carefully track their results, and help them make corrections if appropriate. Budgets and financial reports are included in the reporting instruments.

And there was the failed presidency of Jimmy Carter. He was a lovely, good-hearted, and very luminous Christian gentleman. He and everyone else could immerse themselves into the smallest government and policy aspects but did not forget the electorate recruited him as CEO of the world's largest company, and the big scene was taken away and produced the worst combination of high-interest rates, inflation, and unemployment in our history.

Let's sum up the theory of leverage:

The leverage consists of making money from other people's money and making money from workers, investors, and business associates. You don't have to make money from your brow's sweat.

Although you earn money through sweating, you earn money through the sweat of your brows as they work hard to make you rich.

CHAPTER 5:

They Don't Waste Time On Irrelevant Things

We call millionaire habits profit instead of other habits that contribute to debt and poverty. We call them millionaire habits. One of these habits is the effective use of time. There can be no success without this. Everyone has the same 24 hours, and that's the difference between those identified and those that aren't. Let's see what the millionaires are doing.

Many millionaires have clean desks, while their peers have desks that look like a storm. A safe and respectful workplace is a symbol of organization and order. This means that garbage is collected, and only what is required is kept for that very minute. The remainder is filed off. Clutter reduces time activities because it takes longer to get rid of the mess—the number one millionaire habit is-avoid clutter.

Build a list of tasks

The night before, most millionaires build a task list. This is not done the next morning but is located simultaneously as the alarm for the next day. Some call it the Master List. It is a list of 5-10 main issues to be tackled for the next day.

This "hit the ground running" millionaires as morning arrives when the rest of the world struggles to figure out what the day holds. The millionaire is ahead as they find this out. In comparison to notepads, millionaires often use digital resources such as apps.

Blocks of Time

Millionaires often have the habit of separating the most important things from a block of time. This time block can be between 45 minutes and 1 hour anywhere. During this period, the millionaire makes no calls, goes to the kitchen or even the toilet, and does not even check his email.

The majority of the population, on the other hand, is exposed to distraction, from telephone calls to hours of reading and replying to needless mail, to bathroom and kitchen journeys. So the millionaire is more concentrated and centered in the fulfillment of tasks than the rest of the population, which is afflicted by complacency and decay.

External Source

Millionaires are not trying to do all the job themselves, either. They expend time and have the "SUPER-PRODUCTIVE TIME" It is time for them to make money for others by highly efficient tasks on their behalf. The millionaire also knows that he or she is not successful and happily outsources the other tasks to other people who have a better grasp of them.

To learn the most productive time management and organizational skills, ask a millionaire. That's what I've done over the last few years, and the knowledge I've been receiving is invaluable. I had the fortune to become friends, link, and work in my hometown of Dallas, Texas, with millions of people. Here we've got a lot of millionaires! Dallas alone has more than 70 thousand millionaires.

Over the years, I found some parallels in time management and organization among the millionaires. In their lives, millionaires build order. The order encourages increased concentration, innovation, and productivity. You seldom see the home or workplace of a millionaire dirty and full of clutter. True, they usually have workers to look after the stuff, but many millionaires had those qualities before they were rich.

Millionaires know how time is worth and how best to use it. They understand how to control their time efficiently is essential to the life they desire. One day over lunch, a friend commented on me when he said, "I don't believe in doing volunteer work for charities." The expression on my face seemed to be very puzzled with eyebrows and jaw lifted.

My first impression, I must say, hasn't been a good one. Instead of spending time volunteering for a project, which could save or raise several hundred dollars from the charity, I can put the time into making better use of it and ten times the sum and giving the money." Then I understood.

Even if I'm not promoting this strategy for everyone, it makes sense for someone with this millionaire's potential to make money. Yes, time is money, and you will have a hard time growing rich if you don't manage your time well.

Here are some of the best time management tactics I've heard from millionaires:

- Email: check and respond just twice a day to emails. Email is one of our day's greatest time thieves. Email is never so urgent that it can't wait for a few hours. If so, then a telephone call is more meaningful. I'm just around 10 a.m. checking emails and at 5 p.m. again.
- Phone calls: Like e-mail, answering, and returning at scheduled times of the day. Tell your assistant or receptionist to answer calls and tell callers when to expect a callback. Leave a voicemail message on your cellular phone telling callers that you will answer calls at a certain time of the day. Give them a hidden secret ring code" if you worry about family members or close friends who are having an emergency and cannot contact you.
- Ordinary mail: mail on the same day that you open it. One millionaire said he reads and treats mail as long as he gets it and throws the rest away, so his desk is clean. If anything can't be done every day, have a calendar filing system. Don't

set it aside, put it off, or put it on your desk side. That's a mental diversion. You know that you have to deal with it at some stage in the back of your mind, and it always builds up. Deal with it, do it, and you can move on to something else.
- Clutter: Build order in your surroundings by making them unpleasant. Holding your office, desk, and home free will build an incredible productivity space. It's an integral component of time management because you lose valuable time and concentrate when you can't find what you need.
- To make lists: take a month in advance to write a "to-do" list. Break the month into weeks and then divide the weeks into days. Create a list of priority things the day or evening before. It also helps to predict how long each item will be finished.
- Chit Chat Office: Don't have an "open door" policy for your office. Instead, establish a certain time of day when coworkers or workers may stop talking or ask questions. This removes distractions so you can concentrate your energy where it is most important.
- Come to the point: learn to get to the point without going on any crazy tangent and motivate others to do the same politically. When you're known as someone who doesn't waste time talking idly, others will probably follow your pace. The same applies to telephone calls. Keep short of them and keep them to the stage. My father is an expert. I never knew my father to spend more than 5 minutes on the phone in my life.
- Delegation: delegate, delegate, representative. Nobody else can do better as you do, as one millionaire put it so beautifully.

While it might appear some of these techniques are tough or even unfriendly, the effect is less tension so that when communicating with others, you can be more engaging and less distracted. All should handle their time more productively. Millionaires use that skill to concentrate on the broader picture to their benefit.

CHAPTER 6:

They Don't Avoid Risks

People who want a lot of money are working hard. Rare exceptions exist for those who inherit their wealth, but if they do not have the work ethic to match the money, they normally waste what they have. Maybe that is why milliardaires like Bill Gates continue to operate, while they could live in the interest of money that they already have comfortably for the rest of their lives.

Besides working hard, those who are rich know how to take chances. You start a company, create a new product, or think outside the box. They often don't start rich; at first, they will pay very little for long hours. You're not giving up on your goals, and it pays off. Not everybody who takes a risk is paying as much or even millions as a billionaire on the Forbes list. Most rich people are willing to take a risk.

It has been said since time immemorial that there is no substitute for hard work and commitment. When these two factors are met, every person can accomplish more than they have set out, irrespective of the intelligence or expertise level.

There are hundreds of cases where hard work is worthwhile in more than one way. Every sector has a success story to praise. Don't be under the assumption that success is short. Naturally, you have to find the short cuts when it matters most day and night.

However, some useful tips and secrets are offered to achieve their stage by self-made millionaires. The first and foremost tip of such effective people is hard work. This element carries a great deal of weight and can break down barriers that ever lead to success.

The second most important factor for the self-made millionaires to succeed is their risk. Not everyone is willing to take chances due to the number of obligations he or she has. A study shows that four out of every ten people, regardless of their industry, are willing to take risks.

This pattern is becoming more important, as more people are eager to take chances to achieve success. However, the secret to success depends on a person's wise moves. When taking chances, people should also have options if anything goes wrong. You should also be able to minimize the chance of nullification.

Let us take investment in a product business, for example. The product can succeed or flop depending on the preference of the consumers. Two factors need to be analyzed here. It depends on whether the product has grown in line with customer requirements.

It must also be verified whether the product contains a local material. A product can only thrive in a market if the degree of localization is greater. This is critical because product localization is the key to success. If the product backfires, then you should have ample coverage to resist the effect of future losses. Effective entrepreneurs have taken this strategy to achieve much in different stages.

Innovation is the next key to success. In any undertaking, the creativity quotient must be very strong. There is no reason why a consumer should buy it because a product is revolutionary. There should be a single point of sale in the product that should draw customers' attention.

Once the quotient of creativity in the product is well known, more customers would naturally search for the product. The invention must not be limited to a product that can also be used in different processes. Advancement in a process-oriented industry will make the enterprise a huge sea of progress in the long term.

How to risk your financial life dream?

Many people dream of getting rich "one-day" while others hope to get lucky by winning a lottery while some ladies' dream is to marry a rich man to invest his money, and others are "courageous" enough to engage in illegality and believe it's the way to " quick riches."

Obviously, it is easier to make your money the right way with legal means, but it's not just better; it's much simpler too! Not so "quick," however, but a lot easier. Returning to the "getting lucky," please remove this poor thinking from your mind and remember that the rich don't get fortunate; the rich build their luck. To begin your financial independence journey better, you have to decide where you wish to be and work towards it in five years.

Do you need encouragement to start?

A few millionaires must be there that you know at this point - maybe not directly, but from the news, tabloids, financial newspapers, etc. - and that you respect or want to look "in the future" Write down their names — three rich people at least.

Start by researching these millionaires and begin to examine them. Google your stories, learn how you made your first million, why your second or third were easier to make, what your breakthrough was, what mistakes you made, and how you handled the mistakes. Learn what their journey was. If you want to be rich, there's no better way to get inspired and motivated.

When you do this little job (I may call it a task at all when you learn from experiences and see how their acts are essentially successful (their lives today), when the answers you get from their history are provided to your inner questions, you realize that you are more ready than you planned to climb to the heights of success, as the path forward is clearer. It would be much simpler to draw up a strategic plan for your breakthrough.

As we must take this next important step (whether we learn a lesson or two from a particular millionaire, write down these basic objectives, even if we are not sure how we are going to accomplish this, come up with a strategy, etc. and as we aren't millionaires (yet!), I will not take account of all or rather most of the main aspects of the way millionaires function, but I would insist on one thing, which undeniably helps bridge millionaires: risking.

A millionaire sees a chance where a poor mind sees a danger. For example, millionaires borrow money—millions—to expand their companies and make them even more money. Poor people would rather open a savings or fixed deposits, which is the name of interest simply pays them peanuts.

What can make you furious and hopefully motivate you to take action is that the money you borrowed from millionaires is the money you worked so hard to get the bank to take over. The bank has no capital!

Without your precious savings, the bank will have nothing to loan the millionaires, or rather, detectors for opportunities. So the banks are making their profits – they tax your money, your savings, through their interest. This is not to deter you, not at all, from having your money in the bank. Instead, it is to inspire you to do as millionaires do. Put your money, not just for others to work for you.

Like I did, you can start small. As you become more and more confident — and capital, of course — you get whatever amount you want from your bank or your company. You will have choices!

The development of wealth is a dream shared by many. We want to be stable and have a decent life that will encourage us to have our own homes, have annual festivals, shop if we like it, send our kids to private schools, and retire before the rest.

Even though this can sound like a high order, because the creation of one's wealth entails financial risks, it can be achieved. It is possible to become wealthy if we combine hard work, good planning, and discipline. It also helps, of course, to know the common mistakes and risks to be monitored so you can prevent them as much as possible. Several examples are below:

1. Selecting incorrect financial institutions. Creating wealth requires a strong and secure financial institution, in which your capital will not only be protected but will rise to a respectable level of interest as long as it is retained. Proven banks don't pay very high-interest rates, while relative entrants are all too willing to lure depositors with higher rates and very little stability guarantee.

Owing to their lack of track record, there are financial risks when hiring a new face" in the industry. Try making multiple inquiries at various establishments to get the best offer for your money. Create a comparison chart to help you choose the best possible banks.

2. More debt to repay an old debt. Learn how to repay debt with any income you can produce. Don't hope for a quick payoff by obtaining another loan to repay the other debts.

If your new debt is not free of interest, it will not build good wealth to gain extra debt. Just focus on paying what you owe right now. If you need any compensation leeway, get in contact with your creditors. If you explicitly explain your income constraints, you can understand your situation.

3. Until you can make investments, do not do due diligence. One example of wealth creation investment will be mutual funds. Before investing your hard-earned money in a mutual fund, you first need to scrutinize what commodities, bonds, and shares are bought in the common pool with your financial advisor.

Though mutual funds offer liquidity, diversification, and good management of investments, some funds charge investors high fees. So the important thing to remember is to do your homework to decrease your exposure to financial risks.

4. Debt not due on time. You may think that a $15 repayment per month on the credit card is trivial enough, but the reality is the late repayment fee might be higher than the refund itself! The combination of late fees and interest on the balance at the end of each billing period can easily kill your wealth creation efforts.

Not only that, but the higher interest rate can also be penalized for criminal account holders if repayments are continually missing for months. These are the financial risks you have to worry about in dealing with credit cards or small loans.

5. Don't research enough when applying for loans. Many people regret that they easily took out a loan before shopping for others. A one or two percent difference in the annual rate might seem small at first, but you will realize that the one or two percent could translate into hundreds and even thousands of dollars that you could have saved and put into your wealth creation account.

Don't rush too fast to amass money. The wealthy and prosperous people did not achieve their wealth overnight. It took years of careful preparation, saving, and several years of discipline.

CHAPTER 7:

They Don't Pursue A Goal Without A Driven Purpose

The chapter explores just what mechanisms most millionaires use to turn their finances fully around, from debiting close to half a million dollars to being well on the road to the Internet millionaire and how you might do the same.

The first step – Your goals are not enough

Everybody knows that you need to concentrate your efforts to accomplish something; however, many people make the mistake of keeping their aspirations and future visions in their minds, a position where their hopes and dreams have to compete for space among daily priorities.

To concentrate on your priorities, you must first determine precisely what they are and then establish a spot where they can be consulted regularly. Let them down on paper, in other words. People who are not used to do this make me a little dumb, but high-ranking people know that it is an important move.

There may be several steps between your aspirations and where you stand, so it is important to divide these ultimate goals into smaller goals so that your progress can be easily measured. The advantage of plotting your momentum is that you are given the impetus to conquer the unavoidable challenges life creates.

I recommend that you first write down long-term goals, such as where you want to be and what you want to accomplish within five years, and then work back until you write down what you want to achieve each month of the year.

This takes us to the second stage:

The second step is to educate yourself: Success leaves clues, and there are no better people to learn than those before you. Do you want to hear from someone who wrote about a book that theorizes how to smoke or someone who has abandoned the habit?

If you want to develop wealth in your life, it will be easier to limit your time relaxing passively, such as watching TV. While it can be an excellent way to blanket the world and your issues every day, it doesn't help you produce the results you want.

By minimizing the time you spend on nonproductive past times and increasing the time you spend on your potential success, you narrow the distance between where you are now and where you want to be.

The third step - Have a Regular Schedule

Most millionaires used a regular to-do list, which is another important step in your road to success. This can be a tough habit, but you need to persevere because regular lists are powerful to get over the number one enemy. A daily checklist will assist in setting deadlines because, as an author or journalist would undoubtedly confirm, it is almost difficult to finalize any project without specific deadlines.

 Now you have goals, and you know how much you want to do every day.

What's next, then?

Step 4 - Provide a Structure

We have found that providing regular task lists is as important as setting goals, and all of these are reinforced by knowledge from other effective individuals. --However, this last move seems to bypass most people and is perhaps the most critical of them all. If you want to use the internet to add or even substitute your full-time income, you must know exactly what to do each day to achieve your income objectives.

That's evident, okay?

6. Yeah, some people don't. I have lost the number of people who lament how long they struggle to make money without online businesses' success. If you take the time to see exactly how you spend your time, it becomes clear why you struggle.

You must ensure the mentor's services first-hand or through an educational course or product because that alone saves thousands of hours trying to find all for yourself. The mentor or product that is best for what you want to do online is equally relevant.

Does your strategy include corporate marketing, or do you want to make your products?

Perhaps you want both to master. Whatever decision you take, you can start a successful online venture by taking these simple steps. For all of us, priorities are an important aspect of our future planning. They inspire us, keep us focused on our aspirations and ultimate goals in life, give our actions a specific meaning. However, it is useful to remember a few aspects as we begin to formulate our goals.

Let's remember five considerations when setting goals:

- First, it is important to be clear that our priorities are ours. Many are highly motivated in their early years to receive the praise and acceptance of important adults in their lives. As they grow older, they may continue to live with the thinking and work hard to fulfill their parents, sisters, families, and teachers' wishes.

Over time, you will understand that your driving factors don't have anything to do with your life dreams and that you pursue other people's different expectations and wishes. Although it's nice to be the first person in your family, neighborhood to study and become famous, you need to be clear that that is what you want. Be adamant about the right thing for you.

- Set goals that add meaning to your life, expand your life, and provide a sense of fulfillment and intent. You may want to be wealthy or famous, but sometimes the most successful people are the ones who enjoy what they do and can work hard and long, often with no immediate reward or results. Their motivation comes from their passion, affection, and willingness to understand their efforts' long-term benefits.

- Respect what you have in your life and are inspired to boost your standard of living and your quality of life. Unhappiness also leads to a pessimistic attitude as we reflect on and spin on our lives' poor areas. It could mean that we lose sight of the significance of the people we meet along the way who have had previous experiences.

Respect friendships between past and present, people who assist, inspire, and support you. Enjoy each step of your journey, the difficulties you face, the skills you master, the different ways you learn to manage and overcome challenging situations.

- Give yourself credit for your accomplishments. Some people achieve one target and start to search for the next idea or initiative immediately. Stop for a moment, and taste every achievement instead of constantly driven, always pursuing the next life challenge. Enjoy valuing every achievement you gain, every outcome you are interested in.

- Be versatile so that if anything doesn't turn out the way you expected or wished, you are ready and able to be open to another solution. Be open-minded to the bigger picture, willing to see the potential for exciting, fascinating, and important opportunities to present themselves along the way.

Do you need to go straight from A to B? It may be that you want to be focused on the main target and choose to resist other options; you may consider them as a diversion and not of especial interest to you. However, some people can appreciate the opportunities to be versatile and relish the variety, fascinating detours, and unforeseen mini-successes that occur along the way before achieving their ultimate success.

You will be shocked by how many people live each day without any sense of intent or significance - they just go from day to day, same stuff different day - same habits, same results, and same activities. There is nothing wrong with routine, but the question is - are your routines leading you to greater satisfaction, achievement, contentment, and results?

If they are - go for it - keep at them, but if they are not - remember that maybe your big challenge is seeking and living for a greater intent, one greater than yourself!

Intent - the reason for which something happens or for which it has been done or made, the objective or desired result of something. Without intention - and it can be anything - we are doomed to live a life of emptiness, uncertainty, dissatisfaction, remorse, aimlessness, and stress.

What is the purpose?

In a nutshell, it is a theory that decides or is the benchmark for all of your actions and decisions. You cannot always make the right choices or take the right actions, but when you do not know anything about the incoherence, that is the outcome. But it is like a road map (I know I should say Google here). You know the location, and the map provides you with potential routes and determine which routes to take, considering your time, resources and

Wishes

You can choose - you can take the shortest path, the safest route, or the route that allows you time to enjoy the countryside and the journey - but you have this option essentially. The goal is what motivates you and keeps you focused.

It guides you through hurdles, failure, vulnerability, and challenges. He becomes your best friend when you hear his advice. You should listen and heed his messages or go your way, motivated by fear, greed, the need for validation, or your arrogance, but again. A life without intent is essentially just that – a life without direction, clear goals, and faith that leads you to unknown places in which you sometimes want not to find yourself.

How do you build your intent (discover)?

How do you live with intent every day (moment)?

How do you proceed purposefully when you are bombarded regularly with unknowns, confusion, and problems?

I have found that coping with these external matters will always be more complicated without a sense of intent and will lead over time to more or even the same stresses.

How do you build your intent (discover)?

A lifetime target should not be picked easily or with a limited or casual assessment. It should be built according to a careful study of your hopes, wishes, and what your life stands for. Your current situation, responsibilities, resources, situations, abilities, experiences, or wishes or requests of others do not control it.

But it is not an objective but the basis for the objectives you set and work towards, but it is built from deep within your mind and soul, taking into account the path ahead, irrespective of your present time or circumstances.

No matter how well established the intention is, it is impossible to know what the future holds. Life is full of confusion and endless challenges. The goal is to help you manage them with passion, bravery, confidence, and trust, and these take time to cultivate and display.

By listening, watching, paying attention, and awareness, you find your intent and when it comes to you, trust me - you'll know if it's going to talk to you.

How do you live with intent every day (each moment)?

First, you have to sink deep into your subconscious to remember you at any moment when life continues to question you - are you living for this reason now?

You must then find the courage to achieve this goal, regardless of your circumstances and others' denial, counsel, criticism, or suggestions. The next step is to use your intent as a guide against all your decisions and acts - do I live with this purpose, or is it just a sentence?

You will not change it as the years go by concerning your mistakes or achievements. None of these are simple tasks, but you can eventually arrive at your desired destination with inner happiness, appreciation, enjoyment, and calmness.

How do you proceed purposefully when you are bombarded regularly with unknowns, confusion, and problems?

Life is unsure. We will surely face challenges and trials. These are not intended to weaken us but to reinforce us - the question is, what are we doing with them? Traversing tough times without intent is like moving to a destination that doesn't know what or where the destination is.

A crucial task required to (live) your purpose is to surround yourself with people who believe in you, help you, and want your goals and dreams to be realized. You must also hold validating facts to help your journey in your mind. This means a life full of learning, development, and exploration.

CHAPTER 8:

They Do Not Blame Anyone For Loss, Mistakes, Or Weakness

Another top secret of millionaires is their ability to take responsibility for all their decisions. They do not blame anyone for loss, mistakes, or weakness.

You can find that all of them revolve around guilt if you listen to a lot of conversations. Most people blame someone or something else for their present condition; it could be the boss, coworkers, neighbor, teacher, baby, or spouse. This is the fault of a bad economy. Very few see their actions and decisions as to the root cause of their problems. Let's consider three main ways to get away from the blame and take responsibility for your actions.

Take possession of the circumstances you are in

The easy way to go through life is to blame everyone but yourself for all your problems. It is faster and less stressful to do this. It is difficult to accept that your actions are the origin of where you are now. '

Today, however, is the total of all the actions you have taken up to date. Take possession of the circumstances in which you find yourself. You and you can just change your behavior.

If there is a problem, why not find the solution yourself?

Why not do it yourself if anything has to be done?

You are far less irritated if you take care of what irritates you in any particular situation and avoid waiting for someone to act.

Avoid waiting for something or everyone around you to change

You can only adjust yourself and how you react to any situation. Nobody else can be compelled to adjust. If you don't like everything around you, take steps to change it, if you can, or change how you answer it. You get nowhere to complain about it. It is just an event that generates results

Stop dreaming and hoping, but do something about your life

You don't care and want to get somewhere. I even suggest eliminating from your vocabulary the sentence 'I want.' It doesn't get you anywhere. If you want something, then make a plan, set a goal, and take certain measures to achieve it. This is the only way.

What kind of life would you like to lead?

Would you like to spend the rest of your life wanting different things and complaining about what didn't happen and what didn't happen yet? Do something about it!

Make yourself accountable. Think of the millionaires who realize that their success is dependent on their acts. They don't stand around having 'pity parties,' but they're doing what they want to do. Stop concentrating on your problem. Concentrate instead on finding answers and solutions to your problems.

Move away from the blame game and instead become an active player.

Become involved, be responsible

Actions on our current life station include taking responsibility for our current situation. When we understand that we are the key perpetrators of where we are now, we are more likely to take responsibility for the future that we want.

Most of us grew up without understanding how to take responsibility for our situation. There's always someone else than us to blame. We're playing the game of blame. We blame our families, employers, the economy, government, destiny, the devil, and others for our misery.

We've got hopes, but we're not preparing. We don't implement it when we manage to prepare. Among the few who carry out their plans, most give up in the first regression. We have ready explanations for why events have proven counter to our standards. Most of them return to the Boulevard Status Quo and Grumble-Ville.

You still pass this burden to someone else by refusing to take care of your situation to fix our problems. It is not up to us to repair it. It's someone else. We're waiting and waiting. We are waiting for the solution rather than actively searching for one. We are reactive rather than constructive.

You're still out of the wallet at Broke-Ville, for example. Your take-home pays you off in the middle of the month. You live to check to pay. It's not your fault in your subconscious. It's your boss who declined to hire you or lift you. The weak economy, high-interest rates, inflation, oil prices, or politicians are all about it. It's always your fault.

How are you going to change your situation?

Yeah, because it's not your fault, the other guys have plenty to do. Wage raises promotion, reduced wages, low oil costs, lower bills, cuts in taxation, debt relief, etc. If all fails, win the lottery! You need to get the right cards, and then your dreams come true. It'll get better, sure, one day.

Naturally, liability should be avoided. However, the sad thing is that if we fail to take responsibility, we give our lives and chance to others. When we begin to take responsibility, we begin to do something to manage our finances, create several revenue sources, network, build, and realize our dreams.

In every country, you have those who get battered and battered, regardless of the general outlook, by the economy's vagaries. There are always risers and losers, winners, and losers; it's not about the whole scheme, but about individual scenarios. It is the total of the scenarios which paints the picture of the whole economy.

Let's use the stock market as an example. The prices of certain stocks increase daily on the exchange floor, while others decrease or stay the same. Some stock prices, therefore, rise every day while some fall.

The interplay between bulls and bears gives the overall index course, which goes up or down. This does not imply that all stock prices fall one day and start climbing the next day. Of course, a bear market will trigger dimness and cause rising stocks to decrease, but this does not mean that all stock prices move in the same direction.

For example, blaming the economy is, therefore, escapist. A millionaire is made every day. We have to determine which camp we belong to, winners or losers, bears or bulls. This duty cannot be left to circumstances, time, and chance. We are solely responsible for where we are now. Our current status is the product of prior decisions we have taken. Today, our future is shaped.

I know many people who want to start a business. I always get the same response every time I ask them why they haven't started, lack of start-up money. You need so much money, but nobody can borrow from you, friend or foe, banks are impossible, etc. The tale ends. You just leave it there.

It's not their fault that they haven't begun. It's always an uplifting job to convince them that money is a concept. The reply lies in them—a lot of roads to Rome. Many choices are available for starting a company without mega dollars. Your imagination is the limit.

We can't blame past abuses, skin color, poor luck, and many other things where we stand right now. Our full responsibility is how we react to any adversity we face. It's not an excuse for doing the wrong things. We can't do everything wrong and blame the system for our lack of progress. You haven't done that to the system. Your brain did not shut down; you did.

If we continue to blame external circumstances, we are stuck in a rut and downhill. Pause a moment and take a good look. You will find out that others have moved on in the same situation. What appears to be your hurdle has become a step for others.

The best revenge is a success. Unfavorable circumstances should make us higher, not drown in depths of selfishness. Our attitude and perspective determine whether unfavorable circumstances make us better or more bitter.

Life's not fair; it was never, it's never going to be. Nobody said it was. Nobody said it was. You don't get what you deserve in life; you get what you're negotiating for. Instead of jerking at your cards, work hard, play before an as shows up, and then make good use of it. Luck smiles at those who are willing to pick up opportunities when they come.

It begins by assuming responsibility for our actions, responses. If anyone gives you a negative comment, you have plenty of options. Curse back, smiles, and run, go ballistic, and so forth. You can't force the other party to get upset; you choose.

Our decisions decide if our dreams will come true or not. Let's chose to take responsibility for our lives. Consider past mistakes, live with them, and move on. You are the reason you are jobless. You are the reason you are broke.

You are the reason:

- You are trapped in the rat race
- You have not started the project or business.

- Your dreams have become a mirage. You are the man! Look no further.

Become pro-active.
Get to work.
Dream again.
Study
Prepare and execute.

Before long, you will figure out that you are far away from where you started. It begins by accepting responsibility.

What if I told you that even without looking at your business, you might better your business?

Here is the trick. Practice this clear, realistic method and render incredible forces. You're going to grow and evolve, and you're starting to see your company expand and evolve. This approach produces results without fail every time.

As you absorb this knowledge, prepare to move away from your everyday routine and begin to achieve what is unique and incredible. You will meet your goals. You can do wonders. Get who you've been bred to be.

Someone who doesn't turn around but goes ahead

Someone who likes to think about what might be and wishes to do it

Conceive new ways to do better than you have ever done, rather than either march in or polish the edges of what you are good at right now and then look at the miracles.

Accountability

"It is not about thinking that you are taking responsibility for your life, rather it is about demonstrating responsibility through your thoughts and actions."

Responsibility means you are prepared to be your author or experience. You need to take complete responsibility for everything that happens in your life. The most important ethics you can practice is personal accountability. Recognizing responsibility for your life allows you to flourish in several other ways. It is a question of taking responsibility for yourself and your situations by positive thinking, words, and acts.

There is no question of burden, blame, love, remorse, credit, shame, or guilt. These involve positive and poor judgments and decisions, right and wrong, or better or worse. They're not responsible. We also do not realize that we are not responsible for what we have made.

We continue to do what we always did because it's familiar. It's easy. Change is uncomfortable for many of us; we tend to stick to what we know. If you want the attitude of a millionaire, you must adjust.

Welcome her, hug her, hop into her. Or what you don't like will continue to appear because what you attract is what you attract. Take steps instead.

The behavior of not being dependent is a personal responsibility. You alone govern your actions and your fate. Others can't live for you your life. You should seek advice, but remember to decide what to assess. Absorb what is useful and discard any guidance you think varies from your values, including any principles that you might have acquired.

Personal duty has everything to do with your inner direction. All of us are special and what works with one person isn't necessarily working for anyone else. Learn to go inside and contact your higher self.

Learn to make your choices based purely on your values and not on what your family or friends say. Take full responsibility for investigating a problem's root cause. Fix issues rather than just a fast fix that won't last. Personal obligation guarantees not only current satisfaction but potential assurance.

I combined these diverse experiences to create a unique niche that I needed to succeed in my own life. I combined my training with Joe Vitale and others, including my last two years on the internet, with my marketing expertise. Your internal game directly affects your sales. Since mindset and marketing take place concurrently, it makes sense to look at them simultaneously. That's what my goods and services do.

CHAPTER 9:

They Do Not Have A Weak Determination

Becoming a millionaire is, for many young people, a secret or transparent dream. As we know, some people were born with a silver spoon; others were born into millionaires.

If you get a chance to look at their lives, most of the self-made millionaires are college or school drop-outs and come from a familiar history. Now the question is how these people hold their money position?

Apart from commitment, strong determination, hard work, and management skills, few special characteristics are required to become the most consistent millionaire. Love and enthusiasm for capital are the so-called special features, well-known for investment opportunities, ready for risk-taking, and most importantly, to learn and upgrade their economic awareness. Having obtained all the characteristics of a perfect millionaire, it is important to know the market, where the economic figures reside.

Who in the first place are millionaires?

Okay, millions are just people who have chosen the career path as businessmen. In particular, as the population grew, entrepreneurs in the cities and cities being built saw a need for food and other sustainable goods. Most entrepreneurs have been an intermediary, which means that they have bought products from suppliers and sold them to consumers.

Other entrepreneurs have built small production facilities at home and have produced products for sale. As the competition expanded amongst people worldwide, they were financed massively to make them the world's richest people. Every link in the economic chain was crucial to study in this process.

All millionaires must be inspired by what they do. 'Economy' is thus the principal factor. There are five major reasons why millionaires must be economically cautious. You may be one of several millionaires in the world, but only if you know your strength and beyond, you can't join the "red tapestry." Knowing everything about the country's economy is very relevant. It just helps you to expand your career or in a new sector.

To maintain high-productivity sectors: a quality list of the most productive industries needs to be identified, how the competitive advantage can be achieved, and how those needs can be met. By conducting advanced business and economic analysis, millionaires may take the right path to achieve success and prosperity in the industry. There is little to learn about the so-called economy without a pinch of knowledge.

To develop new business models: After deciding on the best sector, it is important to move forward and prepare to start a business. He or she does not want to mislay a millionaire's reputation; it is important to carefully investigate the market and develop a business model that suits the current economies. You can't do what you want without the necessary skills to analyze the current economy even though you are the world's richest person.

A growing number of Americans achieve a millionaire status simply by studying trends and waiting for the future. It takes time and multiple market studies. Economics plays an important role in rapidly evolving market dynamics. Both millionaires must, therefore, be attentive to market conditions where and when the economy changes.

You may be a millionaire in Forbes or even a billionaire like Mr. Bill Gates, but think you know all your hard work? It is important to work directly to get an insight into the economic status. You will never realize that you surely would be compensated for doing the right job. Perhaps one of the world's richest ten people, but remember that you should be economically intelligent to achieve your ambitions as a millionaire.

CHAPTER 10:

They Never Fail To Get Along With People

In America or elsewhere globally, you do not want to believe that you are fortunate, win the lottery, or have a high IQ like the newspapers. Thomas J Stanley, the best-selling writer The Millionaire Mind, recounts a study of 733 millionaires in his book. The survey asked them to assess the success factors of their income.

The survey respondents reported more than 100 success factors to become a millionaire. The interesting part of the survey was assessing the skills sometimes played down by the media. Many of the millionaires from Hollywood are narcissistic and risky people who make their fortunes at the expense of others as they climb the ladder of success.

This is not the truth. Indeed in Dr. Stanley's study, over half (56%) of millionaires thought that working alongside people was one of the main reasons for their economic success. This contradicts the common conviction that I.Q is an important factor in becoming wealthy. Just 20 percent of the people attained high IQ, and just about 10 percent found that attending a high-ranking college was a key factor in becoming a millionaire.

Why get along with a millionaire is necessary

It is quite difficult to succeed without the help of others. I know that most of the wealthy never recognize their accomplishments.

Because nobody is an island socially or corporately or wealth is produced, you need people to succeed in any business.

You must be able to get along with consumers, workers, and personnel. You need your partner's help when you have to work long hours in the initial start-up phase. You have to give way to the attraction, motivation, respect, and growth of key consultants, providers, and staff. The degree of experience you have ultimately decided how much your business is going to grow.

Another important reason is that you have to cooperate with others; the genius of people around you can't be taped into. This is the act of tapping the power of the mastermind. In a spirit of peace between two or more individuals, a collaboration of information and commitment, among others, is the key to the economic achievement of millionaires and billionaires.

To achieve economic stability, Richard Branson and Bill Gates must collaborate with many. One common mistake I think investors do not trust and value the skill of others. That's what I'm supposing to call the "intellectual blindside" This is when you think you are improving your intellect. I know that I have to get along with others to achieve my goals.

How can I begin to create wealth with others?

I conclude that it is best to take account of and take action with the following tips to use this concept:

Build a positive attitude towards others, helping your business, your connections, and your career

Nobody has ever achieved wealth without the help of others.

Take the time to explore and develop relationships with successful people to inspire you to succeed in your life.

Learn to value your employees, suppliers, and vendors; they cannot change everything.

Develop your actions to embrace others and live happily with your friends, co-workers, or partners to allow you to move forward.

Learn how much you can give than you can.

The millionaire's one secret – getting along will lead you to wealth.

CHAPTER 11:

They Do Not Invest Wrongly

Many millionaires earn a lot of money by wisely investing in the right spot. If you want to become an individual millionaire, you know how to make money and spend your money wisely.

The global recession undoubtedly made investments in different financial markets seem to be riskier due to the economic issues that contributed to it. You can learn about large acquisitions, property bust, and double-digit hedge fund returns. However, good offers with potentially high returns are available under all economic conditions. For those investors willing to take more risk for better returns, three high-return investments will be addressed.

Speculation on real estate

Don't let the widespread land foreclosures trick you into believing that speculation is a goner. In any case, the recession has made real estate purchasing more attractive as deals at low prices are expected to sell for a profit in the future. The risks are higher because the immobilization industry bounces back is still in the air.

Yet inevitably, there would be an upsurge in real estate. The challenge is to purchase assets at deep discounts for a short sale or forwarder, lease them, and bid your time until the demand returns. This strategy could yield better returns in the long run than stock trading indexes.

Hedge Funds

In several respects, hedge fund investing is equivalent to a glorified investment club as it has limited restrictions levied by any regulatory body. This is different from the SEC-regulated mutual funds.

Hedge Fund investments can vary from commodities, inventories, acquisitions, and real estate to large investment areas. With some hedge funds in investment banks like Goldman Sachs posting dual-digit returns after commissions, income can be boosted in a recession.

Of course, there are related risks that you can decimate your portfolio by very bad quarters, but during the downturn, hedge funds kill, as they typically have vast sums of capital at hand, and many deals are open. Another huge benefit of hedge funds is that they have beneficial tax repercussions.

Investments in emerging markets

Emerging markets are much better as real estate speculation, and hedge funds are major investments. Emerging markets are the fast-growing economies of foreign countries. Their governments are committed to offering the nation a favorable investment environment – volatile growth rates and increased investment return.

People will normally ask, "I'm still not making enough money from this job, and I have to look or aim for a higher position in my company or with another company that can give me a higher salary" The higher the income, the closer it is to being millionaires.

Yet earning higher incomes sometimes doesn't necessarily make us millionaires. So what is it takes for a person to earn his first million? Is that just what our paychecks say? Is it the number of qualifications in our curriculum vitae?

You can see that it focuses not only on paychecks, jobs, or even the higher studies placed in the millionaires club if we look at prominent millionaires.

Whereas these personal qualifications will provide you with an edge in the millionaire game, there will still be a difference between an individual who owns wealth and a person who still finds the path to wealth. A person discovers that it is not in the genes, the school he has been at school, or even the business he has been working for the last ten years. So, after all, what's the secret?

The key to millions is what credentials the person has at the moment and how he uses his credentials to inflate his bank account. How you get there depends on your spending habits, your investments, and your investment plans. Concerning spending patterns, people prefer to assume that the more they earn, the higher their living standard.

You can wonder, on savings habits, "Are my savings working as hard as I am?"

It might be easier to think twice if you have kept your savings at the right time. The main point is to know which vehicle savings will provide the highest return rate at the lowest risk. Long-term millionaires typically know how to invest and how much they can save.

This should be in line with spending habits. Technically, because a person increases their ability to produce more income by being promoted or landing a better job, the spending habits should be controlled, and investment savings should be the most advantageous.

As far as investment plans are concerned, now that you have saved enough money from all the years for which you work so hard, it is time for you to put your money in investment funds that preserve your hard-earned money and at the same time provide a higher return rate.

The higher the rate of potential return, the higher the risk. Long-term millionaires typically know how much of their funds can be placed into real property, publicly traded stocks and reciprocal funds, and other assets available on the market today to match their funds.

In building wealth, there are several aspects to consider. Like the millionaires of today, they face various obstacles to get where they are now. No plan for creating wealth is ideal. There will be wrong choices, but there will also be good with proper planning. The trick is to find a well-balanced balance of spending, investments, and plans for investment.

People realize that they don't know how much money they had before they started creating their wealth. You know it didn't just focus on your college degrees. These three important factors, along with any qualifications a person has received from his accumulated experiences in his career, will help him succeed.

CHAPTER 12:

They Don't Occupy Their Mind With Misery And Depression

You will find it tough to find a self-made millionaire full of misery and self-depression. Ever wonder why?

Has your mind anything to do with your success? That's what it does!

It's fair to say that the millionaire mind doesn't function like 80% of the population. Most of them are motivated individuals who can only take steps to accomplish enormous goals.

After reading a few of their novels, they seem to see what needs to be done and do whatever is in their way. I appreciate your curiosity about what ticks the minds. You don't know it yet, but you'll know how critical optimism for millionaires is at the end of this chapter.

What if you realized you could not fail. Imagine that some kind of supernatural being gave you the power to succeed. This strong being told you about reverses here and there, but you will finally succeed. It'd be just a matter of time. This is how many millionaires themselves see their ambitions. You have the confidence to accept them as unavoidable. It's almost as if they can see the future already.

Optimism also improves the capacity to adapt and shift direction, an essential ability to learn from mistakes. Optimists don't consider a roadblock as something they can't solve because they aren't born into it. They would see it as a temporary setback, and only critical thought is needed for a solution.

Optimism and excitement go together, too, and this passion is infected. Others will see how passionate and obsessed their idea is. They want to get out of their way to help the person immediately. This is how, without money or resources, people like Mother Theresa might go around the world. Others were ready to support her because they thought she had done something important. The best way to spread this feeling is with passion for infection.

As a leader, passion motivates you to work harder and exhilarates your idea, as though it were your ideas. People want to be part of something that brings meaning to them. The millionaire's mind includes ample hope to affect the very need to contain people deep inside their minds.

They can imagine the result of a particular course. You can see clearly what will happen if you accomplish a goal. Bill Gates is an outstanding example. He visualized every home in the United States as a young man that will include a personal computer with his operating system. This is when computers cost so much that the wealthy and big business could only afford it.

Optimism will contribute to improved health. Health is the first wealth, as the saying goes and optimists appear to be more involved by their very nature. They are more likely to go to the gym and keep going.

Being an optimist takes away much anxiety. Stress is among the most important side effects of anxiety. With low-stress levels, you benefit immensely from the heart and cardiovascular system. You won't have a heart attack; in other words, Intuition is amplified enormously by being an optimist. The millionaire mind can make more educated choices correctly. They can, therefore, decide quicker, and there is no self-doubt.

If you are predisposed to be a pessimist, you will believe you are doomed. This is not the case, however. Studies indicate that it is possible to learn confidence. It's an ability to ride a bike or bake a cake. It just needs practice.

One way you can practice optimism is to track your self-discussion. Suppose you are irritated and find it difficult to perform a specific mission. Remember to convince yourself that you will finally find the answer. Often we don't behave when we may be wrong because we're afraid. Millionaires are behaving. This cannot be emphasized enough.

Yet far more important than acting, they learn from their mistakes when they are wrong. I heard one millionaire say he didn't make a mistake; one way, he didn't learn. A positive attitude

Optimism brings imagination, as well. Since self-made millionaires don't fear mistakes, they are free to build and to imagine wildly. You don't doubt your thoughts, nor do you think nobody else will get it." It's not a mistake. It grows and profits from things that you do wrong. Edison tried about ten thousand times before the light bulb got right. He then discovered 10,000 ways not to invent the light bulb.

How can you learn from your mistakes?

You look at the problem, how you interpreted it, and what you did to resolve it. They then try to see why their actions did not give them the desired results and how they can help solve the same or a similar problem in the future (whether their efforts or others).

These efforts are also almost immediate, taking just a few seconds to think. Often you have to spend a good deal of time researching a loss and energy. It's not obsessed or based on failure; it's Just so that you can change and become more effective.

Here's an example. I made a big mistake recently. I had a massive amount of info, NOT backed up on my machine. My hard disk collapsed. That cost me a great deal: time and money, headache and tension, not to mention but the mistake took me only 3 seconds to learn BACK UP.

(Okay, maybe a little more time to determine which backup device to use, how and why, and to learn more about the recovery of forensic hard drive data.) But my point was I fucked up royally, took my mistake, learned from it, and moved on.

It may seem quite insignificant. It may only seem sensible to people that they learn from mistakes, but you will be shocked how many people repeatedly make the same mistakes. So one thing you need to do to be a millionaire is to learn from your mistakes and failures. If you continue doing the same (false things, you will continue to get the same (non-millionaire) results.

Think of the terms mistakes and failure as a way of not working." Delete from your mind the negative connotation of these words. So, take action, = Do things. When you make a mistake, don't beat yourself for it, not if, WHEN). Develop, get better, get smarter, get wiser. In all areas of your life, you can also apply this to make it happier. Learning from your mistakes can help you become an incredible person.

CHAPTER 13:

They Don't Ignore The Importance of Sowing Seeds

Millionaires have a peculiar secret most people don't know. Exploring this secret is important to your success in your home marketing business. If you want what you never had, you must do what you never did.

This chapter will address this secret, which you will hopefully embrace and enforce. The development of these secret changes would inevitably impact your quality of life and profits!

The secret is that millionaires know the importance of SOWING SEEDS!

Millionaires know that wealth and success are not only without effort from the heavens. Nobody can expect a big crop without seeds needed, and millionaires are looking to plant seeds everywhere. There are various ways to seed your home business, network, or Internet marketing, and here are a few:

Your initial start-up capital is a seed of any dollar. There's nothing you can get, so investment capital is a must-have.

Do you think that no investment is needed to open a restaurant?
A library?
A nail salon?
An animal care service?
A hotel?

There is, of course! Do you think Donald Trump began his first business without money? Of course not!

But somehow people think it should be free to start an ONLINE company! If you start a business," you need to see AS A BUSINESS! There are costs associated with entering a program or organization. Marketing costs are incurred.

You have to advertise your business, and money is involved. For training materials such as books, courses, etc., capital is required. The capital needed to be in your monthly budget is your automated systems, like your autoresponders or your website hosting.

All of these are important for you to operate your online marketing company efficiently. You know these things, and most people who assume they can just plug their name into one machine are already ahead of you, and all of a sudden, money will begin to flow from the sky.

Which organization would give its "members" without effort a bunch of cash?

None, and that's where most people believe they are "scammed." because they think they're not going to have to do something. They figured out that there were still WORK involved, prohibited from Heaven, but they just scammed themselves. HAVE-TO-HAVE is the start-up venture capital! There was a mistake (The more, the better.)

*Note: If there are any online business opportunities or home business services that you can just plug yourself into a free framework or money, start to flood your bank account with STEER CLEAR! RUN! They're packed with shit! *

Other seeds sowed by millionaires are marketing seeds!

You must intelligently seed marketing seeds so that you and your organization can see as many customers as possible. Let's face it.

Until you tell them, no one will know that you or your business/product exists.

The Internet is a world of dog-eating, and you must separate yourself from the crowd. You should be able to learn from your sponsor, your management, your company, and those in your circle the best way to seed your marketing seed. If you do not have a training platform to show you what works in the marketing arena, stay away!

Marketing is something continuous. You can't make an ad, put a website, put a video on YouTube, and wait for the phone. You must be prepared to remain consistent. You have to be omnipresent on the web. You have to plant your seeds everywhere, but it's certainly a phase, so accept it and don't try to get over yourself to confusion. You have to be able to pursue the seeds that you planted!

The seeds are the immediate implementation of what you read. If you are a "professional student" and still read, study, and immerse yourself in everything you can, but you don't do what you learn, you waste time and all this information and hold all these seeds yourself.

You will get 'blocked up' and paralyze yourself with "info overload" and plant the seeds of what you take in elsewhere by applying them immediately. Millionaires do not wait! Millionaires do not wait! They do it! Even if you don't know yourself fully, it doesn't matter. The simpler it becomes, the more you incorporate it.

Your words and ideas are seeds. Your inner thoughts and words are seeds that you plant into yourself, into your world, and into your company. It is up to you whether they are positive or negative. However, do you think Bill Gates was one that said 'I can't' or 'It's too hard?'

Your ideas decide your thoughts, your words determine your behavior, and your actions determine your actions' consequences.

If you want to succeed and accomplish your goals, you must DO these seeds in your head. You have to Talk these seeds into your universe, and in your subconscious mind, you must see them!

For this reason, personal growth is a must. Self-awareness and connectedness to yourself and your (higher) universe are key! There are life's seeds, and there are death's seeds.

What are you going to plant for yourself and your business?

Yeah, there's a risk with seeds, but you need to be relaxed with the risk! It is not possible to make millionaires if they are afraid of danger. Everything worth getting in life is worth the risk to get it.

CHAPTER 14:

They Don't See Failure As The End of The Road

For many, the above question about the title seems quite strange. The next reasonable response from such people will be, how can I inquire on earth how one interprets a failure if we have been conditioned to hate a failure right from our earliest school days? We have learned it from teachers, parents, colleagues, relatives, etc.

Any of these claims is probably the following:

1) "you cannot afford to fail."
2) "You can't get a good job if you fail in school! "
3) "Anybody who fails cannot amount to anything good in life."
4) "You have to get good grades in school to get a good job! "

As we went from graduate school to high school, we always heard the same failure to pass our exams with flying colors. Any of our colleagues unlucky for failure was no good branded and taunted to the school telling them that he or she would never be anything in life.

Sadly, these comments' emotional and psychological impact left some of these people surprised and frightened to believe what they were told to be real. However, a few others, who never acknowledged these declarations, tried to prove anything possible, they won. They did.

Do you question what I mentioned above?

Okay, then, research live history of people like Thomas Edison, who contributed immensely to humanity through many inventions; Robert Kiyosaki, the author of several bestselling books such as Rich Dad, Poor Dad; Cash Flow Quadrant; Retire Young, Retire Wealthy;

Thomas Edison only had three (three months of formal education) and was sent to his home because he could not go to school. Some of the teachers of Robert Kiyosaki scolded him and called him a good thing since he couldn't get good graduations like the top students in his classroom.

May I make one thing clear to you to my dear friend and reader, whoever has failed doesn't understand what it means? As Zig Ziglar says, "failure is not an entity but an occurrence! 'Failure isn't a case, but a mechanism,' says leadership expert and author John Maxwell. "

Both statements were right if you know that as Zig Ziglar has attempted to demonstrate, it is the operation that failed and not the individual. As John Maxwell describes, failure is an important part of the learning process that leads to success.

Successful business people and companies understand the value of seeing success as a continuous process that helps them create new business development ideas. From their experiences, rivals are still thinking about improvement options and will quickly conquer them if they relieve themselves.

It lacks comprehension of failure that leads many people to walk through life in poverty and desire. We see failure as something that should not be part of us because of our incorrect programming from formal education. So if failure comes, we falsely consider it as the end of the planet. A genuine tale is told of a man who has been laid off for work along with others and guesses what? Suicides have been committed.

The irony in life is that failure constitutes a mechanism in which one may gain important lessons by attempting to accomplish whatever they are trying to achieve in life. I don't suggest that one needs to make mistakes constantly in life.

What is important is how you react to mistakes in your mind and your correction work. If you correct the mistake, you cannot make the same mistake again. However, you cannot rule out completely the fact that you are not making any mistakes.

If you make such mistake again, it just shows that you never learned the lesson the first time. Just for that, you shouldn't crucify yourself! Learn the lesson and step on and concentrate on what you want to do. You are gaining experience by making new mistakes and making the required corrections.

That's why we have the very famous saying, "experience is the best teacher." and "Mistakes are the best teachers" more specifically. All told, it is generally easier to learn from other people's mistakes because nobody likes bad news or a disagreeable outcome.

The founder of Microsoft, Bill Gates, addressed the problem by saying Bad news can be disheartening. There's a real temptation to consider when you get news about a product failure.

Bad news can, indeed be devastating. For instance, around a month before the start of her company Mary Kay Ash, of Mary Kay Cosmetics, lost her wife, and the fact that her banker and lawyer told her before to forget her idea. Her husband's death would normally have marked the end of her dreams, but she never gave up, and today, cosmetics from Mary Kay are a household name.

You could and can find a way to overcome bad news or an unfortunate and unforeseen occurrence so the pain will inevitably go away. Many sources exist of unfortunate news or circumstances - the death of a beloved, fails to marry, the loss of a lover during pregnancy, inability to investigate, rape, torture, armed robbery assaults, company failures, expulsing from home, work losses, dismissal by people you are searching for skilled assistance (e.g., music producers, publishers), etc.

Any of these events leave deep wounds. However, if you carry on with the experience, it will just intensify your mind's scar. One way to let go is by remembering and understanding that the world has not ended for you, that the circumstance or occurrence has taken place.

The suffering is only temporary and will gradually pass away. Moreover, you then continue to actively try to get beyond pain by blocking the pain of the experience and concentrating on a solution.

Microsoft founder Bill Gates does not defeat business people. You learn from it." This is because, as he also revealed in his book Business @ the Pace of Thinking, Microsoft has had its share of product failures, and the useful lessons gained have been used for developing new products.

When you understand the importance of honest mistakes and learning from them, the word failure becomes entirely new; not as something bad but as something you come across on the road to success.

When we speak about someone who has expertise or who is an expert in a field, it is important to remember that the individual has not become an expert through positive events alone.

In the event of negative events, learning and making the necessary corrections, the individual becomes an expert to find solutions to similar or related problems in the future. This is exactly how consultants appear in every industry. They were able to learn from their failures and others and show others how to solve problems.

You must change your view of failure from now on if you intend to do something with your life. Shift the false impression of failure as something you were subjected to at all costs at the formal school and by every other person you ever knew.

Using failure as a method or process from which you learn lessons gives you the requisite experience to become a successful person in your life. Remember, when you encounter events categorized as failures on your journey to success and beyond, you must never let them overthrow you because you need the lessons they hold. What you should concentrate on is a solution to the problem.

I sincerely say to you, and often there is a solution to the dilemma if you look past a failure and try to find a solution and today, please start to teach others what you have just learned about the failure to help reverse the wrong beliefs most people have.

CHAPTER 15:

They Do Not Hesitate To Take Needed Action To Retain Momentum

I have been fortunate to spend time with a few people with great financial and conscious knowledge. This has changed my personal life and the way I do business.

When I heard these people speak and watch how they approach their personal and business lives, I was able to look at three very distinct and influential characteristics. If these three features were added to your life, they would create such a drastic difference that all the stuff you want would appear in your life within a short time.

I don't say that lightly; these three Conscious Concepts and may have affected me. I believe - no, I Suspect, if you apply it in your life, you'll be too.

1: THEY "KNOW" CAN build what you want.

Instead of dwelling on what they don't want, aware millions choose what they want. They never spend time thinking about what their life "missing" Rather, they pick what they want in their lives.

Millionaires believe the rule of attraction 100 percent. They do not doubt that they can build what they want. They don't "believe" they don't know. There is a world between "believing" and "knowing" There's no question when you "know the truth about everything. You've got 100 percent confidence.

I know that you are the only one who knows what is best for you, that you can handle everything and have a good view of your intentions or the result you want to achieve. It is a good first step to be transparent about your intentions. Still, a powerful and life-changing phase is that such intentions are ONLY a reality on the non-physical plane of consciousness and cannot occur in your physical reality unless you hold opposite thoughts.

And then, "Act As If." now is a fact of your intentions. Not dishonestly, or without the true faith, but to experience it, feel it, imagine how it would "show up" as it manifests in your life in different circumstances.

As I watched Millionaires, I saw that they did not hesitate to move on to their ideas and respond to circumstances that needed action to retain momentum.

Are you gaining the strength of this principle?

If you're waiting for anything to happen, doing other "important activities will yield the results you want instead of those you know, you're wasting time, and you're not close to your wishes. It's the habit that you urgently have to develop to get where you want to be! Waiting isn't going to do it!

I saw those Millionaires taking immediate action one after another, not out of fear or pressuring something to take place. Still, because they took them one step closer to their desire with the next action and in their lives, I saw incredible results. They take no unnecessary action. Instead, they use the energy leverage, the same energy leverage that produces all of the universes.

It is time to Get Moving" trust your instincts, realize what a next move is an act. We always wait for the "feeling to be right" first before taking the steps we know will satisfy us. This is backward! This is backward! The sense of fulfillment comes only from Achievement, not from thoughtfulness or delays. (You already knew that one, did you not?!)

Never try to force something to happen because you are afraid of what will happen if you don't act. Instead, pick 'inspired action,' which will take you to what you want, not what you do not want. Action on your intentions without attempting to push anything on would magnetize your expectations by drawing into real people, places, and opportunities that you would never have seen if you had not done so.

Most millionaires cultivate an 'attitude of thankfulness.' Thanks, need no clarification - you know how to be thankful, but did you know that gratitude gives you more?

Thanksgiving speeds the manifestation of your wishes. If you find things you enjoy and use as your focus, your world must change in all aspects of your life. Millionaires conscious realize that they draw more of what they want every time they fill their minds with gratitude or appreciation.

Now, look around you. What would you thank for?

Create a list.

Get into the real sense of true appreciation.

Find anything, something, for now, to be thankful for

When you are glad, you have a strong pulse of energy that attracts more to be thankful, and more positive things come to you magically, attracted by the feelings of appreciation.

CONCLUSION

Are you in the corporate world and have a business of your own?

Are you a blogger trying to do good homework?

It can seem almost impossible to determine how to turn your company into several million dollars if you don't know where to start. However, you can now use the attraction law to help you achieve this goal and advance your business.

Although you might think it will work without you doing too much more work than you are, you don't have to. However, the first step is to start living a millionaire way of life. Here are some lessons from the men who made millions of their own to launch you.

Milliardaires like David Cheriton and John Caldwell have a hair cut at home, for example! Instead of going out and buying costly things, settle for something less expensive. Although getting money means you want to spend anything on it, don't be tempted to do so. This will only finally leave you at one square: broke.

You should love your company or your work, too. The richest people are here because they enjoy their work and do what they do. Concentrate more on doing good rather than concentrating more on creating a good company. Build a business from what you enjoy and love to do.

You will find that the more you like your job, the more you want to work. That was just what Paul Burford thought about when he traded hair crimpers on his website. Paul says, "You're fearless when you're young." This is a positive thing. You draw success when you think you're going to succeed. If you concentrate on being a millionaire, everything else will come into place.

You will have to feel that the company is already one million dollars. Think how natural it is always to have money pouring into you. Regardless of how you use the law of attraction, you have to be careful. Patience is also the secret to a happy and healthy business and personal life.

You have to realize that running a corporation takes a long time, whether you have a home company or own a real office building. You have to do some things, and skipping ahead will not get you anywhere.

The rule of attraction can also be used to help you find motivation rather than items to be sold. The legislation will help you find your niche and make your own business as a blogger, a journalist, or as soon as possible with your store – multi-million dollars.

www.ingramcontent.com/pod-product-compliance
Lightning Source LLC
Chambersburg PA
CBHW070816220526
45466CB00002B/678